friendship @ your fingertips

Monkey Mischief

Written by Tori Kosara

Penguin
Random
House

Senior Editor Tori Kosara
Designers Stefan Georgiou and Thelma-Jane Robb
Jacket Designer Guy Harvey
Pre-production Producer Siu Yin Chan
Producer Lloyd Robertson
Design Manager Guy Harvey
Managing Editor Sarah Harland
Publisher Julie Ferris
Art Director Lisa Lanzarini
Publishing Director Simon Beecroft

Reading Consultant Maureen Fernandes

First published in Great Britain in 2019 by
Dorling Kindersley Limited
80 Strand, London WC2R 0RL
A Penguin Random House Company

10 9 8 7 6 5 4 3 2 1
001—314131—Feb/2019

www.dk.com
www.fingerlings.com

A WORLD OF IDEAS:
SEE ALL THERE IS TO KNOW

**The item should be returned or renewed
by the last date stamped below.**

Dylid dychwelyd neu adnewyddu'r eitem erbyn
y dyddiad olaf sydd wedi'i stampio isod.

PILLGWENLLY   CENTRAL

2 4 JUN 2019

1 9 AUG 2019

− 2 SEP 2019

− 7 AUG 2019

− 5 FEB 2020

To renew visit / Adnewyddwch ar
www.newport.gov.uk/libraries

Contents

3

Melody Village

Welcome to Melody Village.
Monkeys, sloths and unicorns
live in this town. It is a great
place to live!

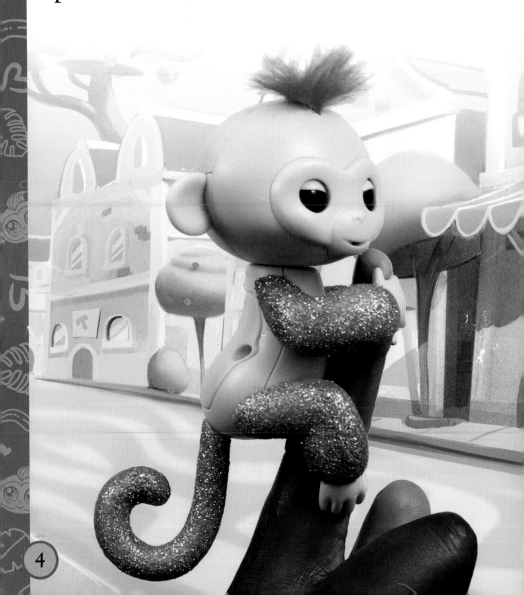

Big town
Explore Melody Village.

The Vines
The monkeys live high up in the trees.

Home sweet home
Some animals live in houses like this.

Sparkle Heights
The unicorns live in a
land made of sweets.

Clubhouse
This big tree house
is fun to play in.

Monkeys hang out in the Vines. They live in tree houses. They climb up to their homes. They speed down slides to go out. Whee!

Monkeys visit the sloths.
They surf together at Sloth
Beach. It is a nice place.

The unicorns live in Sparkle
Heights. Bushes are made of tarts.
Trees are made of lollipops.
Monkeys like to eat these treats.

Meet the monkeys

The monkeys have a lot of energy.
They swing, dance and bounce.
The monkeys can be loud and
wild. They all love to have fun.

Bella

Mia

Boris

Finn

Sophie

Zoe

Sugar, Rose, Kiki and Amelia are sisters. They are the Glitter Girls. They have sparkly arms and legs. The Glitter Girls sing together. Their voices are so sweet!

Rose

Sugar

Bella and Boris are sister and brother. They are twins.

Bella is kind. She is a good friend and a good sister.

Boris wants to be a rock star. He is trying to make his dream come true. Sometimes his plans get him into trouble.

Having fun

These are Bella and Boris's favourite things to do.

Bella

1. Bounce
2. Make friends
3. Tumble

Boris

1. Talk
2. Play the drums
3. Be loud

Finn is fast! He loves to race.
Finn wins a lot of races.

Zoe swings on branches all day.
She hangs upside down. It is fun!

Mia explores. She wants to learn about everything around her.

Sophie is so sweet! She gives her friends big hugs.

These monkeys like to giggle.
Eddie tells funny jokes. Summer,
Charlie, Sydney and Candi giggle.
Hee, hee, hee!

Summer

Eddie

Candi

Charlie

Sydney

25

Ava

Emma

Melon

Monkeys are good dancers.
Hop and spin with Emma, Ava
and Melon. Ava can even dance
upside down.

Busy monkeys

Monkeys are playful. They are always ready for fun. Milly and Willy go up and down on a see-saw.

Milly

Willy

The monkeys and their friends have fun at the Banana Shack. They enjoy banana treats. Candi and Charlie think about what treats to get.

Candi

Charlie

Go bananas!

Try these treats at the
Banana Shack.

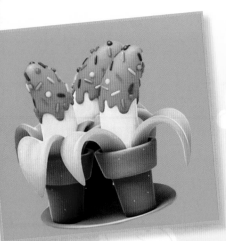

Banana cones

Banana lollipops

Banana slices

Banana milkshakes

BANANA SHACK

The monkeys ride the Daisy-O!
The big wheel goes round and
round. Razz and Quincy will go
for a ride.

Razz

Quincy

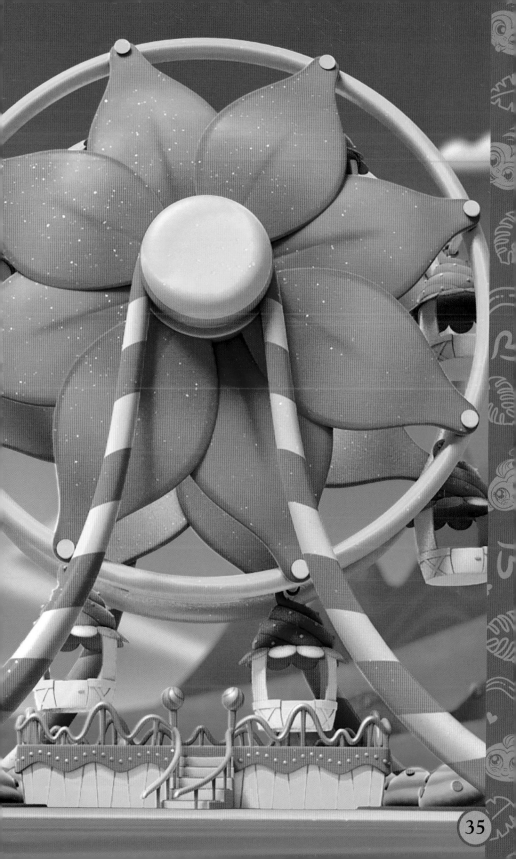

It is fun to go to the playground.
The monkeys can climb high.
Aimee climbs to the top of
the climbing frame.

Look out for the Minis! They are sneaky and fast. The Minis take treats from other monkeys. The Minis like bananas.

The monkeys play pranks
on their friends. Simona rides
the swing. Liv hides on the ladder.
What trick will she play on her
friend? Look out, Simona!

The monkeys are tired. It was a busy day. Some monkeys lie down. Others hang upside down. Good night, monkeys! They will make more mischief tomorrow.

Quiz

1. What type of house do monkeys live in?

2. What are the trees in Sparkle Heights made of?

3. Who are the Glitter Girls?

4. Which monkeys are twins?

5. What does Boris want to be?

6. Who is fast?

7. What do Milly and Willy ride?

8. Where can the monkeys enjoy treats?

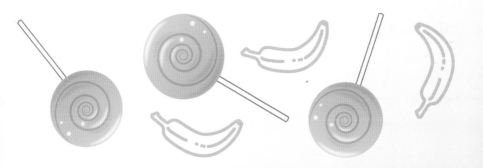

9. What do monkeys play on their friends?

10. Who likes bananas?

Answers on page 47.

Glossary

energy
The power needed to do something, such as move.

explore
To look carefully at something in order to learn more about it.

mischief
Trouble that is not meant to cause harm.

prank
A funny trick that does not hurt anyone.

rock star
A famous performer of rock music.

sneaky
Acting in secret.

tumble
To roll one's body across the ground or through the air.

twins
Two babies who have the same mother and who are born at the same birth.

wild
To have no rules or control.

Index